Escape From the Nazis

ESCAPE FROM THE NAZIS

Gertrud Englander & Bonnie Dwork
with Johnny Dwork

Copyright © 2021 by Johnny Dwork

All rights reserved. This book or any portion thereof may not be reproduced or used in any manner whatsoever without the express written permission of the publisher except for the use of brief quotations in a book review.

Printed in the United States of America
First Printing, 2021

www.EscapeFromTheNazis.com
Contact: info@EscapeFromTheNazis.com

Names: Englander, Gertrud Trude, author. | Dwork, Bonnie, author. | Dwork, Johnny, author.

Title: Escape from the Nazis / Gertrud Englander & Bonnie Dwork with Johnny Dwork.

Description: Includes bibliographical references. | Portland, OR: Peak Experience Productions, 2021.

Identifiers: LCCN: 2021907727 | ISBN: 978-0-5784356-2-6 (paperback) | 978-1-7370510-1-5 (ebook)

Subjects: LCSH Englander, Gertrud Trude. | Englander, Otto. | Dwork, Bonnie. | Englander, Anna. | World War, 1939-1945--Personal narratives, Jewish. | Holocaust survivors--Biography. | Concentration camp inmates--Germany--Biography. | Dachau (Concentration camp) | Kristallnacht, 1938. | Holocaust, Jewish (1939-1945)--Germany. | Jews--Germany--History--1933-1945. | Jews--Persecutions--Germany. | Children of Holocaust survivors--Family relationships. | BISAC BIOGRAPHY & AUTOBIOGRAPHY / Personal Memoirs | BIOGRAPHY & AUTOBIOGRAPHY / Jewish | HISTORY / Holocaust

Classification: LCC D804.195 .E54 2021 | DDC 940.53/180922--dc23

THANKS

Deep bows of gratitude go to Alexa MacDonald for editing this book and Lieve Maas for its graphic design. Many of the amazing family documents in this book were generously provided by Paul and Michael Israel and Don Gordon. And a tip of the hat to David L. Phillips for your consistently wise counsel.

INTRODUCTION

Those who cannot remember the past are doomed to repeat it.

–George Santayana[1]

These are the stories of how my mother's family miraculously escaped the Holocaust. My grandparents, Gertrud (Trude) and Otto Englander, and their two daughters, Anna Englander and my mother, Bonnie Dwork, were fortunate to survive. Growing up I knew little of their experiences leading up to and during the war. I only came across Trude and Bonnie's first-hand written accounts when I was going through my mother's papers after her death.

Trude and Bonnie never publicly promulgated their firsthand accounts of persecution and escape. However, given the recent global rise in xenophobic populism and authoritarian leadership, I am quite sure they would approve of this book as an investment in the prayer: *Never again, never again, shall any human deny the Holocaust. Never again, never again, shall there ever be another Holocaust.*

Escape From the Nazis

On Adolph Hitler's orders, the Nazis systematically murdered at least 10 million innocent civilians because of their perceived "racial inferiority" or political differences. This included more than six million Jews as well as Roma (Gypsies), Slavic peoples (Poles and Russians), Jehovah's Witnesses, homosexuals, communists, socialists, and the mentally and physically disabled.

Every one of those 10 million souls had a mother who labored in pain and love to bring them into this world. And to what end? To be heinously tortured and then brutally murdered out of pure, unbridled, opportunistic hatred. How could such utter madness have existed?

My family was relatively fortunate; only a few of us died at the hands of the Nazis. As Hitler rose to power in the 1930s my elders scattered to the four winds: England, Uruguay, Israel, and America.

Upon reaching New York City, my grandmother and mother built new and prosperous lives. My grandmother became a much-loved teacher of pottery at the famous 92nd street "Y" in Manhattan. My mother married a benevolent New York doctor, birthed me, and then became a social worker specializing in the support of Holocaust survivors living in New York City. In that role Bonnie also served as one of the interviewers for the "Survivors of the Shoah" Visual History Foundation.

Introduction

As was the case with so many who escaped the Holocaust, my mother was determined to raise me in a "safe nest" that would shelter me from the type of persecution she experienced when she was a child. Accordingly, I grew up feeling safe enough to become an adventurous lover of life, spending my days making a living as a producer of the celebratory and visionary arts.

As I grew into adulthood I learned about the horrors my family had endured. Witnessing the rise of new genocidal atrocities, I began to see that along with the freedoms I enjoy comes a moral responsibility to do my share to prevent such injustices from happening to others.

In turn, several realizations have motivated me to produce this book:

First, my grandmother and mother were good-hearted, honorable people whose presence made our world a much better place. By sharing their stories I honor my elders, Trude and Bonnie, for the light and love they brought to this world.

Second, I want to help people understand how the Holocaust happened and why, even after those horrors became widely known, additional genocides have occurred. The Czech author Milan Kundera wrote, "The struggle of man against power is the struggle of memory against forgetting."[2] It astounds me that Holocaust deniers still exist. Even worse, few people understand how the seeds of genocide are planted and nurtured in the minds of a populace. Gertrud and Bonnie's stories chronicle those gradual changes in public sentiment and illuminate how genocides like the Holocaust start.

Third, the historical parallels became undeniable as I watched the 45th president of the country I call home build support for his authoritarian aspirations fomenting xenophobic divisiveness and encouraging a murderous mob mentality among the masses. Knowing that this playbook has led to genocide in the past, I could not remain silent.

Perhaps Pastor Martin Niemöller's quote says it best:

> *First they came for the Socialists, and I did not speak out —*
> *Because I was not a Socialist.*
> *Then they came for the Trade Unionists, and I did not speak out —*
> *Because I was not a Trade Unionist.*
> *Then they came for the Jews, and I did not speak out —*
> *Because I was not a Jew.*
> *Then they came for me —*
> *and there was no one left to speak for me.*[3]

Introduction

Early Warning Signs

My grandmother wrote that in the beginning of the Third Reich my grandfather did not believe Hitler, with all his petty divisiveness, rampant lying, and warmongering, could sway an entire nation to risk everything in the name of hatred. But Hitler *was* successful, and he rose to power by systematically undermining the social and political infrastructure.

Just as Hitler did, contemporary politicians denigrate the media, polarize public perception through constant fear-mongering and lying, politicize domestic security agencies and use them to spy on and harass domestic political opponents, use state power to reward corporate backers, stack the judicial branch with pro-authoritarian judges, enforce the law for only one side, purge voter rolls, and, as has been done since biblical times, blame minorities, immigrants, and refugees for all the nation's challenges.

> *People can always be brought to the bidding of the leaders. That is easy. All you have to do is tell them they are being attacked and denounce the pacifists for lack of patriotism and exposing the country to danger. It works the same way in any country.*
>
> –Hermann Göring at the Nuremberg trials, April 18, 1946[4]

Escape From the Nazis

Journalist Shawn Hamilton writes:

> *The faulty premise that empowered Hitler and helped place him in the German mainstream was called the Dolchstoss or the legend of the "stab in the back." It argued that, despite all of the evidence to the contrary, Germany was winning World War I only to have politicians surrender prematurely. Hitler, as a political figure, was the embodiment of this hack theory. While many rejected Hitler's anti-Semitism and bellicosity, his deep sense of having been wronged by Germany's surrender in World War I...gave him authenticity. It also created a hole in the German Republic's legitimacy that he and his followers barreled through.[5]*

In the United States today we see many examples of Dolchstoss, ways in which the populace is encouraged to feel betrayed and aggrieved — the stab in the back. One example is the suggestion that illegal immigration is the cause of the economic struggles of white working-class Americans when, in actuality, mechanization, globalization, weak unions, and poor representation are more to blame. Another example is the questioning of the trustworthiness of our elections and, thereby, the legitimacy of the elected government. The world has seen this before. We know where it leads.

INTRODUCTION

Can We End Genocide?

Common sense dictates that humanity should have learned the stark and terrifying lessons of the Holocaust. But apparently not, for the twentieth century is referred to by many historians as the "century of genocide."[6] And so far, in the 21st century, we are on track to equal the previous century's grim record. Since the end of World War II, genocides around the world have resulted in at least 2.4 million deaths.[7,8]

International organizations such as the United Nations have developed guidelines to prevent future genocides. These top-down strategies are useful to deter regimes that are already exhibiting genocidal behaviors. However, societies as a whole, from the bottom up, must address the fundamental root causes of genocide. Prejudice and hatred are not genetically inherited; they are learned.

Accordingly, humanity must proactively commit to fostering in each new generation a global mindset of holism, cultural tolerance, and empathy. If we are ever to evolve beyond this sinister mindset all democratic societies must commit, in perpetuity, to teach every new generation about genocide and how to prevent it. And, as the past few years have urgently revealed, we must strive to reclaim the "post-truth" social media environment that has recently run amok with unchecked, fear-inducing propaganda and conspiracy theories.

Escape From the Nazis

Consequently, we must teach media literacy. We must give future generations the skills they will need to recognize and reject the seductive messages and propaganda of dominator cultures that divide and conquer. We must provide them with an education that nurtures compassion and inclusion. And we must recommit, again and again, to institutionalize a robust grassroots rejection of racism and systemic oppression.

Personally, sharing my family's history becomes part of a diverse action plan that invests in a better future, one in which truth and justice prevail over ignorance and prejudice. And so, here are the extraordinary stories of a family that experienced the buildup to genocide and then, miraculously, escaped the Holocaust.

In light and with love,
Johnny Dwork

Please see resource section on page 63.

Notes

1. https://en.wikipedia.org/wiki/George_Santayana
2. https://quillette.com/2019/03/31/historical-amnesia-and-kunderas-resistance/
3. Niemöller, Martin. "First they came for the Socialists…" United States Holocaust Memorial Museum. Retrieved 5 February 2011
4. https://encyclopedia.ushmm.org/content/en/article/martin-niemoeller-first-they-came-for-the-socialists
5. Gilbert, G.M. Nuremberg Diary. New York: Farrar, Straus and Company, 1947 (pp. 278-279)
6. Hamilton, Shawn. "What Those Who Studied Nazis Can Teach Us About The Strange Reaction To Donald Trump" *HuffPost*, 12/19/2016 07:13 pm ET, https://www.huffpost.com/entry/donald-trump-nazi-propaganda-coordinate_n_58583b6fe4b08debb78a7d5c
7. Bartrop 2002: 522
8. https://en.wikipedia.org/wiki/List_of_genocides_by_death_toll
9. https://ourworldindata.org/genocides

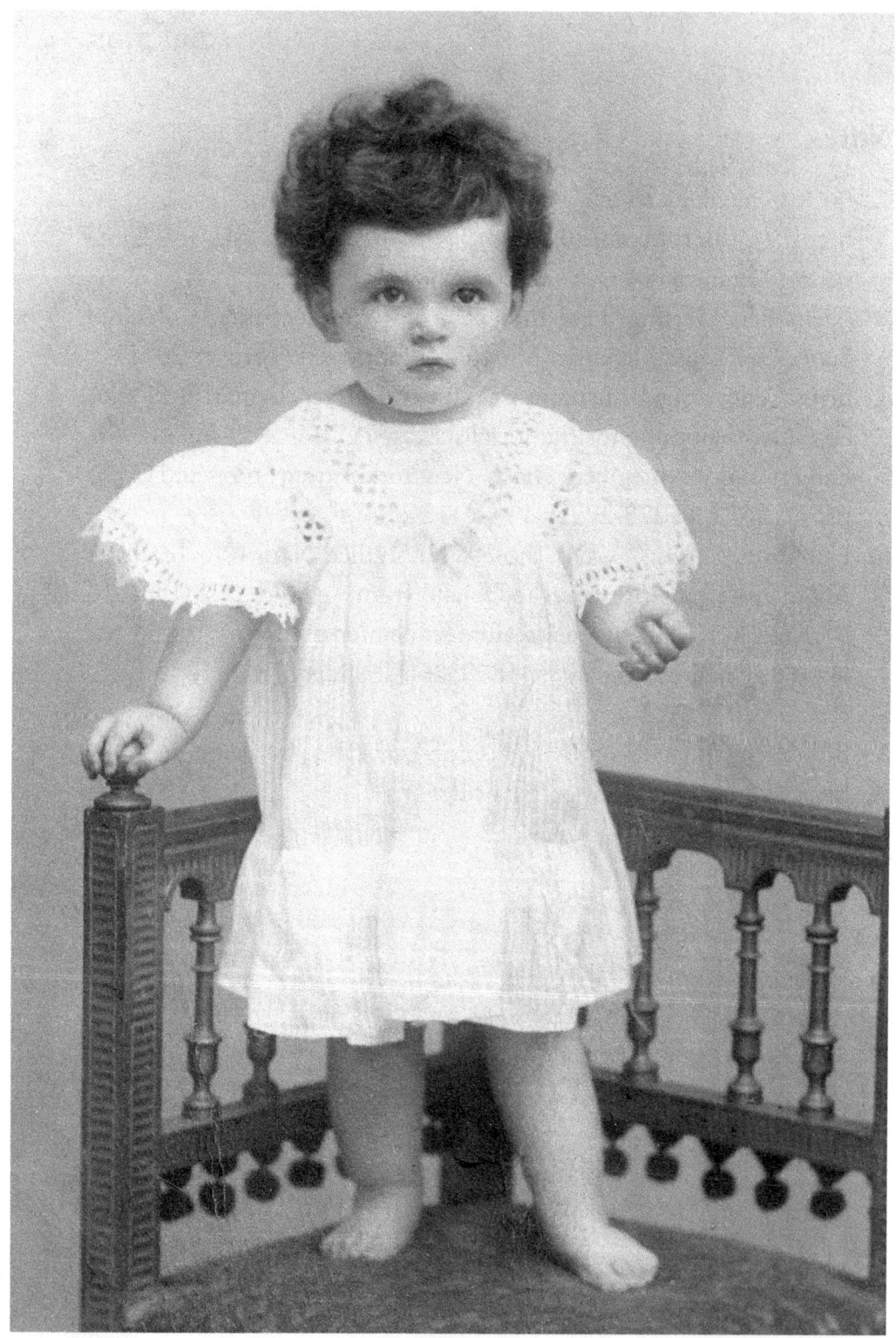

Trude, 1905.

Sig, Thea, and baby Trude.

GERTRUD'S STORY

I was born in 1904 as Gertrud (Trude) Israel to Isaac Israel and Frieda (born Mändle) in Sontheim-Heilbronn on the river Neckar in Germany. Sigmund (Sig) was born 10 years before me, Therese (Thea) was eight and a half years my senior, and Louis came one and a half years after me.

Sontheim was a village with about 5,000 inhabitants. It was close to Heilbronn, a city of 45,000 at that time. My father was a partner in the Mechanische Schufabrick, a shoe factory which my grandfather, with his three sons and a son-in-law, had founded around the turn of the century. The factory kept about 1,000 workers employed. Of course, many of the workers came from nearby villages and towns. There was a streetcar from Heilbronn to Sontheim and a spur of railroad from the former to outlying villages and towns.

Sontheim had a handful of Jewish families, all middle class. There was one Jewish doctor, and there was a small synagogue in the village. On top of the hill, above the shoe-factory complex, there was a beautiful home for the Jewish elderly from the whole state of Württemberg. My grandfather and my father, together with other Jewish industrialists and philanthropists of the State, had been involved in the founding of the home. We were a well-respected family, and my father was, for several years, an elected "Gemeinderat," a town elder. When my grandparents celebrated their golden wedding anniversary the whole village celebrated with us. The evening before there was a big festival in the gardens with lights strung out under the trees and bands serenading the guests. All the athletic groups sent their deputies to congratulate the couple, and the king of Württemberg sent a delegate with a sculpted, gilded portrait of the king and queen. On the anniversary morning when the family procession—my grandparents had 11 children and many grandchildren—proceeded down the hill to the synagogue for a service, the church bells of both the Catholic and Protestant churches rang.

Golden wedding anniversary, June 23, 1912.

Heilbronn House.

My grandparents lived in a beautiful two-family house with their oldest daughter and her family. The house (above) is now designated a landmark because of its architecture and stained-glass windows. It stood at the entrance to the shoe-factory complex surrounded by beautiful gardens. Before they built the factory, my father's family had come from Hohenlohe, not far away.

We lived in the village in a two-family house with my maternal grandparents, and we had a garden there too. My mother was born in Sontheim. My maternal grandmother was a Rosengart from Buddenhausen in the Schwäbische Alb. Her family had some vineyards and some land and, before retiring and selling out, had owned a tavern in Sontheim called the Gasthaus zur Traube (Inn of the Grape). My mother was much loved by the people. She always brought meals to the poor and the sick.

Friede and Isaac Israel.

Louis and Trude.

I had a sunny childhood, enjoying the countryside and the seasons, the river nearby. My friends were mostly the Christian children with whom I went to school in Heilbronn. I did not experience much antisemitism although there was an undercurrent of it during the reign of the emperor. During the First World War everybody was very patriotic and involved in the war effort, and we had many projects to help. I remember taking care of small babies whose fathers were in the war.

After the war, when my grandparents had died and my father was semi-retired, we moved to Heilbronn where most of the family lived. There I got into a circle of young Jewish people and became more active culturally and socially.

Portrait of Trude as a young lady.

After the war the political climate became very chaotic with the pendulum swinging back and forth wildly. There were leftist, rightist, and democratic governments in quick succession. There was inflation for many years. The index changed dramatically every day. A lot of people, especially white-collar workers on fixed incomes, became impoverished, and small businesses crumbled. Hitler tried a coup in 1923, but it was unsuccessful, and he went to prison.

Trude and Otto.

Gertrud Israel Englander

I was married in 1925 and moved to Stuttgart where my husband Otto was born. He owned a factory with his two younger brothers, Ernst and Walter, and a cousin. The factory, Gebrüder Englander, had been founded by his father and his uncle. They manufactured all kinds of curtains. They also had a weaving mill in Saxonia which is now in the Russian Zone. There they made lacy materials called English tulle.

By 1930 we had two young daughters and had a very modern house built according to the Bauhaus ideas. The house took a year to build, and during this time politics became very critical. The German people were depressed following their defeat in the First World War. Hitler had come out of prison, and his ideas gained strength. He made the Jews the scapegoats. When he became Chancellor in 1933 he made the first law against the Jews: Jewish businesses were to be boycotted, and Jews were to be excluded from banking and cultural activities as well as the Universities.

1930 - The new family home built according to Bauhaus concepts — the idea of creating a *Gesamtkunstwerk* (comprehensive artwork) in which all the arts would eventually be brought together.

Family life before World War II - Trude and her girls raised an organic garden grown according to Rudolph Steiner's "Biodynamic" principles which were new at the time. Anna would embrace these principles for the rest of her life.

As long as Hindenburg was President he would not allow Jewish war veterans to be included in the restrictions. My husband fought in WWI and received the Iron Cross for bravery. But after Hindenburg died in 1935 the Nuremberg laws were enforced which took citizens' rights away from Jews. From then on the world seemed to stand on its head and life became a nightmare. The propaganda by the Nazis and all their groups became frenetic. The little children joined the Hitler Youth. They marched and sang with their bands and banners, singing those Jew-killing songs all day long.

The radio blared constantly with their speeches and announcements full of hatred. When we had to go to town it was traumatic. We did not dare to encounter one of their groups marching and singing their violent songs. They were everywhere. We would have to salute their flags with "Heil Hitler," and we could not. We had to hide quickly in a dark corner or side street. Concentration camps had been started for those politically opposed and for Jews, and the smallest misstep could throw you in. A lot of Jews left Germany.

My husband and his two brothers had all been in the war and had been honored with all the medals. Otto had been critically wounded toward the end of the war, and it took a year and a half until the big piece of shrapnel which had pierced the main artery in his neck worked its way out. They were all good citizens, and they thought they had nothing to fear. They could not believe what was happening, and it took them a long time to realize that this regime would not blow over. It became more and more difficult to leave.

A Judensteuer, Jew tax, had to be paid, but bank accounts had been blocked, so no money could be transferred. No valuable goods could be purchased. Jews had to deliver all silver and jewelry to the authorities, who melted them down. The most humiliating laws were that our domestic help had to leave us because "Jewish households could not be trusted." It was hard for everyone. After a few unsatisfactory experiences we got our wonderful Josefine. Since we were only allowed to employ the elderly she fitted that category. She even took the girls home to her village for vacations since it was no longer possible for us to go anywhere.

Judenboykott. The Nazi boycott of Jewish businesses in Germany began on April 1, 1933. The signs read: "Germans! Defend yourselves! Don't buy from Jews." Source: Wikipedia and Bundesarchiv, Bild 102-14469 / CC-BY-SA 3.0).

We kept our distance from the neighbors. They were not unfriendly, but most of them did not know about half of the harassments we were subjected to. The children had befriended a little boy next door as soon as we moved into our house. He played with them almost all day when there was no school.

He changed when he joined the Hitler Youth, and his parents became fearful that he would denounce them for being friendly towards us. He threw mud balls into our windows, and painted swastikas and dirty slogans on our wall. I took my heart in my hands and approached him with a bucket of soapy water and a brush. I said, "Harald would you be good enough to scrub it off?" And he did. A few months later when our girls left Germany, he came over the fence at night and brought each of them a doll in a basket.

Hitler Jugend (Hitler Youth) was founded to indoctrinate the German youth with the Nazi ideology while preparing them to serve Hitler's Third Reich as loyal soldiers. By the end of 1933 there were 2.3 million German boys and girls between the ages of ten and eighteen in the Hitler Youth organization. (Source: Alamy).

One woman on our street, the wife of an officer in the State administration, approached me once at the street-car stop. She introduced herself and tried to comfort me, saying that all this would not go on forever. She started a friendship with me, calling me from public phone booths under an assumed name. In the end I left my pearl necklace with her, which I got back after the war. Unfortunately she had died.

The worst came in November 1938: Kristallnacht. All synagogues in the country went up in flames. Windows of Jewish businesses were smashed and the shops looted. The next morning two SS men stormed our door and took my husband away. It became clear during the day that all prominent Jewish men had been collected and taken to concentration camps.

Kristallnacht, (the Night of Broken Glass), was a pogrom against Jews carried out by SA paramilitary forces and civilians on November 9-10, 1938. The German authorities looked on without intervening. (Photo credit: "Kristallnacht Aftermath," by Mike Licht).

Escape From the Nazis

The girls were at school when their dad was led away. At first I did not tell them, but they found out soon enough. These were anxious days and weeks. After three weeks my husband and his brother, Ernst, who had been in a different concentration camp, were brought together at a Nazi party office in the middle of the night. There they were confronted by two Nazis who forced them to sell their two factories very cheaply. One Nazi, the owner of a competing firm, wanted the weaving mill. The other, a uniform manufacturer, bought the Stuttgart factory with all the equipment. Both were high officers in the party; one was a storm trooper.

SS guards force Jews arrested during *Kristallnacht* to march through the town of Baden-Baden, Germany. November 10, 1938 (Source: Bildarchiv Preussischer Kulturbesitz/US Holocaust Memorial Museum).

Then Otto and Ernst were released. Their hair had been shaved off, and they looked so thin and pale. Later on our men told us that the other prisoners in the camps had been sewing yellow stars on the uniforms for weeks in anticipation of the Jews' arrival.

Helene and Otto Wachenheim lived in Holland and were cousins of the brothers. They offered refuge to my mother-in-law, Oma (Fredericke Englander-Herbst); to Ernst, who was divorced; and to Walter, who had been an invalid since the encephalitis epidemic after WWI. So they left.

The girls, who had been increasingly taunted by their Christian schoolmates, were forbidden to continue at school.

The girls, who had been increasingly taunted by their Christian schoolmates, were forbidden to continue at school. We had to send them to Switzerland where my older brother Sig and his family took them in. We could not take them because our passports had been taken away. So Josefine took them. She had an international passport because she had been the personal maid of the Fürstin of Thurn und Taxis (sister of the Emperor of Austria) before she worked for us.

Josephine

Since this passport prevented her from being searched, she took some of my sentimental jewelry pieces and pinned them under her hatband. The really valuable pieces we did not dare hide and had to give them over to the Nazis.

It was very hard to send the children away. We did not know whether we would ever see them again, and they were aware of that too. This was January 1939. My husband was busy finalizing the business sale. Until that was accomplished they would not let us go.

GERTRUD ISRAEL ENGLANDER

Although the workers and employees had been instrumental in instigating the sale, they now behaved as if we were selling them out. It turned out that the money had to be turned over to the unions to protect the workers, and they squeezed the last penny out of the deal. It also turned out that the contract contained a clause that none of the Gebrüder Engländer could ever start a business of this kind again anywhere in Europe.

At the same time we tried frantically to find a country that would take us. The children could stay in Switzerland for six months as a result of a money guarantee my brother put down. He had been generous not only by taking them in, but also sending them to private school since they came in the middle of the school year. He and his good wife, Susi, didn't want them to miss school.

Trude's brother Sig and his wife Susi.

We had permission to go there to pick them up if we had a visa to go on from there. We had an immigration number to go to America which the cousins had picked up for us when they made their final visits to the American Consulate, but this number would not come due for years. Finally, at the end of January, my younger brother Louis called from London to say that we had permission to go there. He had gone there as a young man to be apprenticed to an uncle who had started an import business. Louis was married to Marjorie, an Englishwoman born in South Africa.

We sold the house to the Nazi-appointed buyer, a munitions manufacturer, at the Nazi-decreed price.

We sold the house to the Nazi-appointed buyer, a munitions manufacturer, at the Nazi-decreed price. And, of course, our money was blocked right away. When we submitted the list of furnishings and belongings we wanted to move, we experienced the greatest harassment. Included was a book of stamps, left over from my father's collection which had gone to Sig in Switzerland. They thought we had smuggled valuables out of the country that way. Lots of house searches by the Gestapo followed. Once they got me out of the dentist's chair. The whole thing became a nightmare. Finally, we were relieved to have the whole thing confiscated.

But we still waited for our passports. My husband even considered swimming across the Rhine to Switzerland, a highly dangerous project because of the border patrols.

But we still waited for our passports. My husband even considered swimming across the Rhine to Switzerland, a highly dangerous project because of the border patrols. Finally, the passports came at the end of May 1939, and we flew to Switzerland the next day. We had a small suitcase and 10 marks each, our only money. The permit to pack our belongings came after we left, and Josefine and our faithful dog, Astor, supervised the packing. But the furnishings never made it to us because war broke out. Much later we heard that they were auctioned off to bombed-out people in Bremerhaven.

Living room in the Stuttgart Bauhaus.

We were reunited with our children in Zurich. Then we flew to London via Amsterdam where we saw Otto's mother, Oma, and his brothers for the last time.

We were reunited with our children in Zurich. Then we flew to London via Amsterdam where we saw Otto's mother, Oma, and his brothers for the last time. In England we could breathe more freely, but in September 1939 war broke out, and we were considered enemy aliens.

When Hitler invaded Holland we got permits from Bloomsbury House (the Jewish organization that helped us get to England) for Oma and the brothers to come too. We sent one telegram after another urging them to come, but never got a response. We were without news from them until we came to the States.

Because of our enemy alien status Otto was not allowed to work, and they came to intern him in one of the camps they had set up for this purpose. However, by then our number had come up for the U.S. and our passports were at the U.S. Consulate. So they said they would be back for my husband in a week.

The miraculous reunion in Switzerland.

Escape From the Nazis

We had moved out of Louis's house where things were a bit crowded with baby Michael and his nanny, and were renting a typically small house without central heat in a London suburb called Edgware. We were raising a victory garden. The girls were going to a small neighborhood school where they had made friends, and we were happy. However, although Louis was generous, we could not support ourselves, and the bombings got worse. There were many air raids, and we spent most nights with our heads under the kitchen table.

Arriving in England, the Englanders pose with Trude's brother Louis and his wife Marjorie.

We did get permission to come to the U.S. but could not get passage because all the boats were being used to evacuate English children to Canada. So the threat of internment for my husband continued. Then a boat filled with children was sunk by a German U boat, after which many parents changed their minds about sending their children across the Atlantic. So we got passage. The train which took us to Glasgow, from where we were to sail, was stalled in the middle of the night because of an air raid. The Royal Arc, berthed next to our ship, the S.S. Cameronia, was bombed that night. Our crossing took 14 days because the ship took a zigzag course to try to avoid U boats. The convoy which we were promised would protect us, did not materialize. We had to wear life preserves day and night, and there were anxious moments, especially when we mistook whales for submarines.

We arrived in New York on July 30, 1940, the hottest day of the year. But that didn't matter to us. We were so thrilled to see the Statue of Liberty as we sailed up the harbor.

We arrived in New York on July 30, 1940, the hottest day of the year. But that didn't matter to us. We were so thrilled to see the Statue of Liberty as we sailed up the harbor. We were met with open arms by Traute and Karl Herrscher whom we had never seen before. She was a niece of my sister Thea's husband, Arthur.

Bonnie

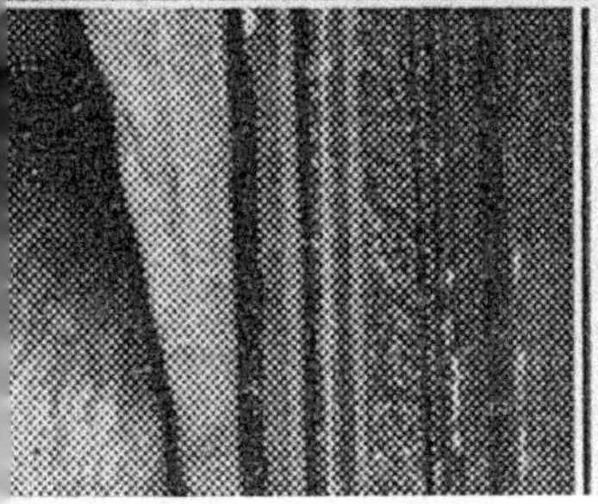

YANKEELAND LOOKS GOOD

British children wave to America after arrival yesterday on the S. S. Cameronia. Aboard was Lady Blennerhasset with her baby boy, born the day her husband, Sir Marmaduke Blennerhasset, Royal Navy lieutenant, was killed in action.

—Story on page 14

Now we could again correspond with the family stranded in Holland. We applied for "First Papers" as our intention was to become U.S. citizens which would enable us to send affidavits to our relatives. These affidavits would guarantee that we would support them so that they would not become public charges. My husband did not have a job yet, but the girls and I earned some money sewing beads on designer hats at home.

Ernst

We were advised to send for Ernst first because he was technically trained in a weaving school and would be considered employable, but Ernst refused to come alone. So we worked on a scheme to get the three of them to Cuba. However, this did not work out, and in the meantime America entered the war. After that we were cut off from them again, and I do not remember the succession in which the bad news came to us.

GERTRUD ISRAEL ENGLANDER

Ernst was deported to a staging camp in Holland called Westerbork. Oma was completely devastated by this. She became irrational and had to be hospitalized. From there she was put on a deportation train that was packed so tightly that no one could sit. Mercifully she died on the train. Walter was hospitalized under an assumed gentile name. After the war we heard that Walter died in the hospital and was buried with his false name just six weeks before liberation. He had been such a sweet patient person. We made many inquiries and finally got a report that Ernst had been sent from Westerbork to Mauthausen in Austria, one of the most notorious concentration camps, where he perished.

Oma

Walter

Escape From the Nazis

We also learned that the residents of the Elder Jewish Home, which my grandfather and father had helped found, were all deported and killed. Among them were two of my aunts, sisters of my father. A younger cousin of mine, Alice Harburger, born Rheinganum, was deported from Ulm with her husband and four-year-old son. We heard that she was shot to death at the site of a mass grave in Riga. We do not know what happened to her husband and child.

By the end of the war we had rebuilt our lives again in a small way. My husband became an office manager in the New York branch of the tobacco import and export business of Otto Wachenheim. The Wachenheims had resettled here from Holland. But my husband could never get over the fate of his family, and he mourned them until his death from cancer in 1956.

Gertrud Israel Englander, June 15, 1987

After the war, a peaceful life reclaimed.

Trude and baby Bonnie, 1927.

Anna and Bonnie, 1935.

BONNIE'S STORY

Kristallnacht

I was 11 years old on that November day in 1938. As the trolley on which I was riding home from school came to a clearing, the whole town of Stuttgart was spread out below us. A passenger pointed down to a large area of fire and smoke and announced that the synagogue had been set on fire. I froze in disbelief and fear. Others in the car were likewise silent. At home my mother not only confirmed what I had seen but added that the windows of all Jewish owned stores downtown had been smashed. She seemed quite subdued. When my father did not appear at the dinner table she announced that he was on a business trip. That was not unusual because he and my uncle owned another textile factory in Bielefeld and he frequently traveled there.

Interior view of the destroyed Fasanenstrasse Synagogue, Berlin, burned on Kristallnacht; November Pogroms. (Source: Center for Jewish History, NYC).

At school the next day one of my Jewish classmates asked if my father, like hers, had been taken to a concentration camp. I could hardly wait to get home to confront my mother who admitted that the Gestapo had come to the house the previous morning at 5 a.m. to take my father away. She had been to Gestapo Headquarters, but they had refused to tell her of his whereabouts.

Jewish men rounded up by the Gestapo in Stadthagen after Kristallnacht. (Source: https://collections.ushmm.org/search/catalog/pa1120169 https://collections.ushmm.org/search/catalog/pa1120168).

There was more bad news. My younger sister, along with her Jewish classmates, had been expelled from public school that day. My turn followed in two weeks when the private school I had been enrolled in since 1933 was pressured to force its Jewish students out. There were no Jewish schools in Stuttgart. It was a relief to escape the constant harassment, both physical and verbal, of our gentile classmates. Our most frequent playmate had been the gentile boy next door. After joining the Hitler Youth he started throwing mud balls through our windows and he painted a swastika on our house. My mother brought out a brush and made him scrub it off.

Propaganda poster from 1935 with the title *Jugend dient dem Führer. All zehn-jahrigen in die HJ* (Youth serves the Führer. All ten-year olds in the Hitler Youth).

The next three weeks were a nightmare. My mother, our relatives, and Jewish friends were trying desperately to learn where their men were and to obtain their release. When my father came home I was in shock. His sandy-blond hair had been shaved off and the stubble that was growing back was gray. His color was ashen, his self-assurance gone. He and his brother had been brought back to Gestapo Headquarters the previous night, he from Welsheim Prison, my uncle from Dachau. Then they were forced to "sell" their factories to a high ranking Nazi, a competitor who had coveted the business for years. Not that the very low selling price mattered, for the money was immediately frozen. Then my father and uncle were released after promising to emigrate as soon as possible. My father could never discuss his three weeks of incarceration.

Since our quota number to the U.S. would not allow emigration for years, my parents concentrated on saving my sister and me. A maternal uncle who was a Swiss citizen offered to take us. When we said goodbye we did not know whether we would ever see our parents again. Our maid, Josefine, took us across the border. She had an international passport because she had previously been employed by the sister of the Emperor of Austria. Because she would not be searched, she offered to pin some of my mother's jewelry inside her hatband. That jewelry, my father's violin, the clothes we carried, and 10 German marks each were the only things we could get out.

It was five months before we saw our parents again. Another maternal uncle in England was able to arrange for the four of us to come to London. My paternal grandmother, two uncles and other relatives perished during the holocaust.

(Unterschrift der Behörde)

Polizeira

A Poem By Bonnie Dwork
Will We See Our Parents Again?

Anna and I are on the train to Zurich with loyal Josephine
who has my mother's jewelry pinned to the inside of her hatband.

Will we see our parents again?

My father, taken to prison on Kristallnacht,
is released and arranged for our departure.

Will we see our parents again?

Tramping through the snow to the funicular
which takes us down to school and back again
to the home of our Swiss aunt and uncle.

Will we see our parents again?

Our parents remain in Stuttgart selling factory and home,
or rather, forced to give it to the Nazis,
so they can emigrate with us to England.

Will we see our parents again?

Italy invades Albania. We are prepared to flee
with our packed belongings if there is war.

Will we see our parents again?

Months pass. Spring comes,
and our parents are on a train to Zurich.

Yes, we will see our parents again.

EPILOGUE

Upon reaching New York City, my maternal family built new and prosperous lives. My grandmother became a much-loved teacher of pottery at the famous 92nd street "Y" in Manhattan. Anna became a Waldorf School teacher, first in New York, and then in Scotland. My mother married a benevolent New York doctor, birthed me, got her Master's degree in Social Work and then became a social worker specializing in the support of Holocaust survivors living in New York City. In that role Bonnie also served as one of the interviewers for the "Survivors of the Shoah" Visual History Foundation.

Johnny Dwork

Anna's graduation.

Trude at the potter's wheel.

Bonnie and Dr. Kermit Dwork.

Bonnie with newborn Johnny.

RESOURCES

- **Directory of organizations for genocide awareness:** https://www.ihgjlm.com/directory-of-organizations-for-genocide-awareness/
- **Genocide Watch:** www.genocidewatch.com
- **United States Holocaust Museum:** https://www.ushmm.org/
- **The World Holocaust Remembrance Center:** www.yadvashem.org
- **Ernst Englander Memorials:**
  https://www.joodsmonument.nl/en/page/207122/ernst-englander
  https://yvng.yadvashem.org/nameDetails.html?language=en&itemId=659366&ind=2
- **Walter Englander Memorials:**
  https://www.joodsmonument.nl/en/page/234871/walter-englander
  https://yvng.yadvashem.org/nameDetails.html?language=en&itemId=687514&ind=1
- **Fredericke Englander-Herbst Memorials:**
  https://www.joodsmonument.nl/en/page/32206/frederike-englander-herbst
  https://yvng.yadvashem.org/nameDetails.html?language=en&itemId=1394751&ind=2

FAMILY TREE

SALOMON ISRAEL AND THE NEXT FOUR GENERATIONS

SALOMON ISRAEL (1838 - 1921) married **BABETTE RHEINGANUM** (1838-1917) in 1862

```
                        > SIGMUND IRELL                        > CLAUDIA married JURGEN CAPITAIN
                        ( (1894-1980)    > WALTER IRELL        (
                        ( married        (  married            > GUIDO IRELL
                        ( SUSI BLOCH     ( MARGRET             (
                        (                                      > THOMAS IRELL
                        (
                        > THEA
ISAK ISRAEL             ( (1896-1983)    > LEA
(1863-1933)             ( married        (
married                 ( ARTHUR HENOCH  (                     > HANOCH married EFRATH ZUNZ
FRIDA MANDLE            (                > ELISCHEWA           > RAYA married ISRAEL BRAMA
                        (                ( married             > YAIR married RUCHAMA BAZIA
                        (                ( SEEF PLESSER        > HILLEL married MICHAL YACOBSON
                        (                                      > BRURIA married ELCHANAN SAMET
                        (
                        > GERTRUD        > BRIGITTE (BONNIE)
                        ( (1904- 2001)   (  married            > JOHN DWORK
                        ( married        ( KERMIT DWORK
                        ( OTTO ENGLANDER (
                        (                > ANNA (HELENA)
                        (
                        > LOUIS ISRAEL
                        ( (1905-1990)
                        ( married 1.
                        ( MARJORIE MORRIS > MICHAEL            > SUZANNE
                        ( (1911-1979) and 2. (  married        > STEPHEN ISRAEL
                        ( SARAH FLACH    ( JUNE CRAFT          > PAUL ISRAEL married RUTH KAY


                        > ERNST ISRAEL
                        ( (1898-1965)
                        ( married
                        ( ROSEL BLAU
ALBERT ISRAEL           (
(1864-1944)             > SOFIE
married                 ( (....-1968)    > GEORGE VICTOR       > EVA
CAMILLE DAVID           ( married        (  married            > JOHN VICTOR
                        ( EUGEN VICTOR   ( AENN LOWENGARD      > TONY VICTOR
```

	> JULA ((....-1970) (married (PHILLIP EISINGER ((	> MARGOT (married (HENRY BAUER	> NANCY married (ERWING MUTH (> JOANIE married (HENRY HINTON
FRIEDA (1865-1928) married RICHARD GIDION	> SIEGFRIED GIDION ((....-1979) (married (GRETL BAUER (		
	> RUTH (married (MAX BLOCH (	> SUSAN (married (HAROLD LOEW	> KAREN (> MICHAEL LOEW

	> GERHARD WOLF ((1900-1984) (married (FRIEDEL FREY ((1881-2000) (	> LILLIAN (married (JOSEPH SHAPIRO	> KIM married MICHAEL (KONISBERG > KEN SHAPIRO married {PATRICIA NASCIMENTO
EMMA (1866-1932) married HERMAN WOLF (1862-1926)	> LOTTE ((1907-1949) (married (SIGBERT GOOD	> PETER GOOD	

	(((> LESLIE ISRAEL (married (ENA EDELSTEIN ((	> PAT (married (TONY HERZ (> DIANA (married (RON LEVIN	> see TONY HERZ > ANDREW LEVIN > SIMON LEVIN > MATHEW LEVIN
ADOLF ISRAEL (1867-1966 married KATIE LAZARUS	> TERESE ((1908-1984) (married (CHARLES DAVID ((1906-1999) ((((	> JOHN DAVID (married (ROBERTA > KITTY (married (WALTER SHERWIN	> LISA married (ERNEST BERGER (> JOSHUA DAVID > MARK SHERWIN (married CATHY > JENNIFER married (DAVID MILKEREIT

```
                        > SIEGFRIED RHEINGANUM
                        (
                        > THEKLA
                        (
                        > BERTA            > KURT JACOB        (
                        ( (....-1966)      ( married           > PETER JACOB
                        ( married          ( REAL MUELLER      (
                        ( JULIUS JACOB     (
                        (                  > GUSTI
                        > ROSALIE
                        ( (....-1971)
                        > ELSA
                        (
TERESA                  > JOHANNA
(1868-1925)             ( married          > RICHARD JACOB     (
married                 ( ROBERT JACOB     ( married           > LINN
HERRMAN                 (                  ( FINNI ROSENWEIG   ( married
RHEINGANUM              > RICHARD RHEINGANUM                   ( 1. FRED POLAK
(1859-1935)             ( (....-1918)                          ( and 2. WAYNE PRESLEY
                        (                                      > GERRY JACOB
                        (                                      ( married
                        > ALOYSA                               ( SYLVIA ARROWITZ
                        ( (....-1943)      (
                        ( married          > HANS HARBURGER
                        ( JULIUS HARBURGER (

                        > JULIA
                        ( (1888-1943)      > MARIANNE          > GEORGE SCHNEIDER
                        ( married          ( married           (
                        ( JULIUS SCHWAB    ( OTTO SCHNEIDER    > JOHN SCHNEIDER
                        (
                        > TEKLA                                > JILL married
                        ( (1889-1971)      > FRANK STEINER     ( ANDREW SOUNDY
                        ( married          ( (1912-            (
                        ( IGNAZ STEINER    ( married           > MARY married
                        ( (1874-1940)      ( JOYCE LANE        ( ANTHONY LAMEY
                        (                  ( (1918-1994)       > CATHERINE married
                        > ADOLF HERZ                           ( REX TORDOFF
BERTHA                  ( (1891-1939)
(1868-1934)             ( married          > PAUL HERZ
married                 ( HILDA GIDION                        > JEREMY HERZ
LOUIS HERZ              (                                     (
                        > KARL HERZ        > TONY HERZ         > NICHOLAS HERZ
                        ( (1897-1981)      ( married           (
                        ( married          ( PAT ISRAEL        > ADAM HERZ
                        ( LEONIE GIDEON                        (
                        (                                      > VANESSA
                        > MINA
                        ( (1896-....)
                        ( married
                        ( SALI FEIBELMANN
                        (
                        > OTTO HERZ
                        ( (1897-1943)
                        ( married
                        ( TRUDE KARLSRUHER
```

JULIE
(1871-1944)

MORITZ ISRAEL   > EUGENE ISRAEL
(1874-1958)   ((....-1979)
married   (
BELLA SILBERMANN >: BEATRICE
(....-1952)   ((1908-1987)
                   (married
                   (1. LEO BAUER and 2. HUGHES WOOD

ROSA
1877-1944

LINA   > CHARLES DAVID
married   ((1906-1999)   > JOHN DAVID see ADOLF ISRAEL above
HENRY DAVID   (married   (
                   (1. TERESE ISRAEL   > KITTY married
                   (and   (WALTER SHERWIN see ADOLF ISRAEL above
                   (2
                   (EDNA MAE DURBIN   > PETER DAVID

Julie, Babette, and Salomon Israel.

Moritz Mandle, and Clara Rosengard Mandle.

The Englander family: Walter, Frederike Engländer-Herbst (aka "Oma"), Heinrich, Otto, and Ernst.

www.ingramcontent.com/pod-product-compliance
Lightning Source LLC
Chambersburg PA
CBHW080632170426
43209CB00008B/1552